I'VE BEEN TRYING
TO LEAVE SINCE
I GOT HERE

By Don Lindsay
Co-Written By Sam La Piana

FORWARD

"There's so many things that happened, you're probably going to have to label this as fiction. People won't even believe it. Though most stories can't be made up, they happened…"

THE NAMES

"Where did the nicknames, Klutch and Norman come from?" I asked. Don responded, "Well, one time we were having a party, we were always having a party, and she was clutching up and I said, 'don't clutch up' and it just kinda got that way."

Don and Ruth- "And then it finally got to the point where we were Norman and Mildred Klutch from Nebraska."

Alan/Knuck- "And then uh Knuck, he was knucklehead."

Susan/Zip- "Zip, she was always talkin', Zip! The lip!"

Linda/Yinner or Yin- "And Linda, she couldn't say, 'Linda'. 'What's your name? My name is Yinda' so finally that turned into 'Yinner' and that's how she got that."

Ray/Cec- "Cec he was Cecil McGillicuddy, I don't know why but he just looked like one."

"Yeah, I nicknamed all of 'em."

For Don, the nicknames weren't just silly names for his wife and kids. Don had the ability to read and person quickly and then sum them up in word or phrase. This word of phrase usually became the nick name. Granted, sometimes it all revolved around an untimely mishap that Don just happened to have witnessed.

GENERAL MISBEHAVIOR

"Charlie and I never woke up in the morning and said, 'Now what can we do to get in trouble today?' It just happened."

When Don was just a kid, about ten years old, he lived in a little house in the City of Leavenworth with his family. This house had a basement garage. At this particular time in history, chocolate was "unheard-of" in their family. Don had been born in '31 and grew up in the great depression. This was a time in America where Don had been lucky enough to get one watermelon a year and he never did get soda-pop.

It was at this time, Don found a box of Ex-Lax, which to him, was as good as pure chocolate (at least in appearance). As he says, "I knew there was something wrong with it, but I had it anyway... ...And we had some garage doors that opened up side-ways to some retaining walls." Everyone had gone looking for Don as he hid behind the walls then pushed into the garage behind the door where he couldn't be seen. It was at this time, Don decided to eat *all* of the "chocolate." Years later, recounting the story to me, Don looked up and smiled as he said to himself through a literal, *shit-eating grin*, "I crapped for a week."

"She was fearless when it came to machines," smiled Don as he recalled Yinner in the shop when he let her saw some stuff once. "Scared me to death."

At one point, Don had a gun that only shot "22 shorts". In contrast, a common type of ammunition is 22 Long Rifle. This is a 22-caliber bullet with a longer casing to allow for more gun powder. "22 Short" is simply a round that has a 22-caliber bullet with a shorter casing that allows for less gun powder. However, according to Don, you could put "long rifles" in the "22 short" gun. This was done by jamming them in and using a knife to pull them out. Naturally, Don possessed this particular gun during World War II when there was a severe ammo shortage, especially for irregular ammo such as "22 short". Finally, Don had found a box of shorts and managed to secure them. In order to save the ammo from being used up, Don would go about jamming the more common and easier to find "22 longs" into his rifle. One day, his brother Charles went out with his gun *and* his shells. Next thing Don could hear was, Boom, Boom, Boom! Don realized what was happening and went running after Charles to stop him from using up all of the "22 shorts". Don still has a bad scar on his leg from hurtling a barbed-wire fence to get after him.

"I had three company cars and they all got in a wreck, and I was out of town!" Don mentioned... Don had a company car that wore out which he turned in and got a new one. The new one was at the house and he had a loaner car while the transmission was being fixed on his old car. As it happened, three of Don's "company cars" were at his house when they 'all got wrecked.' Don's boss called him and said, "Don, I want to talk to you about your company cars. First off, most guys are satisfied with one." Don replied,

"Well, it's a long story." Don's Boss replied, "I got the time."

Don explained to his superior, "Knuck was movin' them for something and he turned too quick and bumped a fender and then when he turned too quick he bumped another and then he…"

"Them little bastards," Don said. "I had some whiskey, the people we went to had some whiskey and Charlie had some beer or something." This was on a hunting trip at a time when one could not purchase beer on Sunday. Sunday also happened to be the day the group drove home. However, the previous night, the boys had gotten into the liquor and beer. After the boys had called it a short day, the group headed home. "Not a drop of liquor or beer or nothin', we drove all the way back, dry" Don said with a look of annoyance on his face. Then his face lightened up as the punch line to the story came, "No jury would have convicted us if we'd have killed them boys."

Once when Don and friends had stopped for lunch, Don ordered first. "I said, I'll have chili," Don said with a smirk on his face. One of Don's friends replied, do we still have the contest on? Don said yes and they all ordered chili. "And I won the fartin' contest," Don said with an even bigger smirk on his face.

"We had a guy we took from work," Don then laughed so hard he couldn't say the next part. After composing himself, Don continued. "He (Al) was so crazy. We got as far as Seneca, which isn't very far, and we already had a case of beer" Don said as he laughed like it had just happened. They were playing poker in the back of the camper while Al was driving. Finally, Al pulled over saying he didn't want to drive anymore. He was tired of the rest of the guys in back having all the fun while he had to do the driving. Don said okay, we'll all just get out and pee. All the guys un-assed (Army term for getting your ass out of a vehicle or seat) the back of the truck and could hardly walk to take a pee. Al grimaced as he shook his head and said, "Well shit, it looks like I better keep drivin' then." "Okay, who's deal?" Don replied.

As Don says, he never set out to start trouble but it sure did find him. Yet another of Don's traits was his ability to take a story an insert it into his formula. Tragedy + Time = Comedy. It is said he had quite the knack for taking something that wasn't funny, and making it funny.

THE GREAT OUTDOORS

"Charlie considered it a party, but I was serious
about hunting. Real serious about hunting."

Once Don and his buddy Charlie went out hunting on open-ing day. Charlie's grandmother lived between the old 24 highway and interstate 70 over near Lawrence, KS where there was a pond that sat about a half mile from the road.

One opening day in particular, Don and Charlie had their decoys set and everything ready to go. From the get-go that morn-ing the two partners in crime began shooting the ducks as soon as they came in. After a little while Don and Charlie saw a game war-den truck pull up. Don saw this and announced, "Uh-oh" to which Charlie replied, "Oh, don't worry about it!" Don looked at Charlie, "You got a license?" "Oh yeah, yeah," Charlie replied. Don moving mentally to the next hot-ticket item asked, "You got a plug?"

(Now, for those of you who don't know, a plug is an item inserted into your gun to limit the amount of rounds it can hold. This is something required for hunting as you are only allowed to have three rounds in your gun at a time and many shotguns hold five or more rounds.)

"Oh yeah," Charlie answered. "Okay then," said Don. As stated, the pond was a half mile from the road, so they had plenty of time to watch the game warden make his way to them. When he arrived, the game warden began, "Hi boys!" After a few simple pleasantries, the game warden stated, "Well, you're in a lot of trouble." Don tried to explain that they both possessed a license and that their guns were plugged and above all else, Don even had a copy of the regulations with him. The game warden appreciated Don had the regulations and recommended Don read them. Don insisted he didn't need to read them, but the game warden insisted more. Don was then guided by the Warden to focus on the shooting hours. Don pointed out the hours being a half hour from sunrise to a half hour after sunset. The warden agreed then encouraged Don to read further. Don began to perspire as he was feeling less and less confident that he and Charlie were in the right. Don then saw the line, "...except opening day, when hunting opens at noon." Don looked at his watch and saw it was ten thirty.

Don and Charlie had their guns taken away which they had to get back by showing up to court in front of a judge and paying a fine.

It should also be noted, in following years, Don and Charlie took an alarm clock with them to be sure they played by the rules. However, their master plans were thrown off by the simple fact they had their alarm clock set wrong.

As a final aside, many years later (after serving in the Army) Don belonged to an armed forces club that flew them to Washington on a fancy plane. The plane had a couple generals on it and even a few judges. With Don's luck, I'm sure you can imagine how it was that Don happened to know one of the judges.

"We lost Charlie one time, out pheasant hunting," remarks

Don. As he explains, this was a particularly weird situation because you could see 5 miles any direction. As the group proceeded
in a line across the field, they suddenly looked around and there
was no Charlie.

They then found out they'd crossed over a dry stream that
was full of tumble weeds. Apparently, Charlie didn't know anything about tumbleweeds, so he stepped on them and disappeared.
The boys then spent an hour or two looking for Charlie. Finally,
they found him by poking sticks through the weeds. "Hell, the
weeds were so bad, Charlie was calling for help but no one could
hear him!" explained Don.

Don, Charlie, and another guy or two were fishing out in
the Ozarks once. In this particular case they were casting for bass
with plastic worms. At one point, one of the guys leaned back
as he cast and caught his hook on Charlie's skull. The man then
went to follow through with his cast, but it didn't cast. The man
thought he had a limb or tree branch, so he started shaking it.
As Don tells the story, laughing, the man began shaking his rod
which got Charlie screaming and hollering. The man finally figured out Charlie was caught with his hook.

Don and the guys took Charlie to the hospital where he sat
for an hour or so in the ER room waiting to get seen by the doctor.
All the while during the wait, Charlie would get irritated by the
worm moving around in his face, so he'd push him to the other
side of his nose by exhaling from his mouth.

"Finally," as Don says, Charlie bought a boat. It was a "Scott-
Atwater, made by SEARS." However, "...the damn thing never did
work right" or at least according to Don, "It always quit on us."
The guys headed out to the middle of a reservoir where the motor
quit but they still were coasting. As they coasted by a tree, Don
instructed Charlie to reach out and grab the tree and hold on to it.
Don added in, "don't lift your foot off the boat!" "What!?" Charlie
asked as he lifted his foot off of the boat. And away Don went as
they left Charlie in the tree.

11

Hindsight being 20/20, Don looks back laughing and says, "I think what pissed him off the most was that I kept fishing." As Don kept fishing, an old man in his own boat came around so Charlie tried to get his attention so he could get some help. However, the old man just ignored him. That afternoon, Don was able to find a guy with a boat who could take him back to pick up Charlie.

One winter it was first ice out and Don, Charlie and whoever else may have been involved went to Tonganoxie lake to hunt duck. At the lake they had 3 or 4 packs of beer, naturally, as it was particularly cold that day. Finally, as it got dark, they decided it was time to go home. It was at this time they had an argument about who was able to drive and who wasn't. Don still isn't sure who "*won*" the discussion but either way, he ended up driving. So, as it goes, Don was driving Charlie's old pick-up. As they went, Don was back and forth across the highway and Charlie finally spoke up and said, "I have to pee." Don told Charlie to wait but Charlie continued, "I've gotta go, I've gotta go." Don finally just pulled the truck over and said, "Go on, pee." Charlie then opened the door and disappeared. Don told Charlie to get back in the truck. After no response, Don looked back but couldn't see anything. Then Don did see, he had come within a foot of a cliff that dropped off twenty to thirty feet. When Charlie made it back up, he said, "I thought I'd never stop fallin'."

All things being equal, when asked if Charlie was okay, Don explains, "…well, he was so loose…"

"We would go to Milford (lake) and I would get up in the morning and go walleye fishin'" Don said explaining how they got breakfast on those trips. After this, Klutch would "ski the kids" the rest of the day. One day in particular, Don was tired. Klutch offered to drive the boat on her own. Don asked if she knew what she was doing and as you'd expect, Klutch said she did. Don agreed so on Klutch and the kids went. Don sat on the shore with his friend Jim and after a short while here comes Klutch, driving the boat, kid in tow, really close to the bank. Don beings waiving, "Get out! Get out! Get away from the bank!" Klutch just waived back. Suddenly, a grinding noise filled the air. "Oh shit, there went the motor," remarked Don. This left Don in a situation. The boat couldn't go forward, and the marina was three miles off. As the universe would have it, the only way Don could drive the boat was backwards. Now picture, Don driving across a lake in reverse in a 17.5' boat. "I'm backin' up, and I feel like an idiot just backin' up in this reservoir, Milford," noted Don. Chuckling to himself, "So I had a rod and reel, so I threw it out and acted like I was back-trolling."

Now, Don told you that previous story so he could tell you another. When using the truck with the camper on the back, and boat in tow, the camper door would not open all the way, due to the presence of the boat trailer. That day on the lake when Klutch broke the boat, someone felt sorry for her and parked the boat at the ramp for her so Don could pull it up. The door had been left a-jar before all the maneuvering. I think you know what happened to the door...

Another time, Charles had pulled Don's boat to the lake with his big Chevy farm truck. This was on 4th of July weekend, so Milford Lake was busy as hell. Don went to use his brother's truck to get the boat out and the brakes locked up on the ramp. For hours people were honking and yelling at Don until finally, a guy was able to drag Charles' truck with Don's boat-loaded trailer up the ramp and out of the way (eventually to a garage, on locked brakes). "That was just another part of another day."

Once Don borrowed Charlie's boat, "A little John boat and it had a 9.5 horsepower Sears motor on it." According to Don, it was a really fancy thing and it even had a little pump on it. The pump would pump any water that came in, out of the boat. Don knew it was time to go when the water got to his ankles. Don would start it up and by the time he got to a new spot, it was dry again.

Don put the boat on a trailer that wasn't made for it and he punched two holes in it. This was the day Don decided to take the

13

boat to Lake Pom Du Tare. They decided to take the boat out any-way but with two big holes in the boat, the pump couldn't keep up. Don's brilliant solution was to put lifejackets over the holes and have kids sit on the life jackets. In true Don fashion, on a day with four kids and two adults fishing from a boat, this was normal.

As a side note, the same trip, Don employed his usual method of getting a beer while driving. They'd be driving down the road with the windows down and kids in the camper. As soon as Don's bottle went dry, he'd reach out the window and above the truck to the camper overhang and thump on the camper. Sure enough, a little hand would reach out the camper window and hand him a beer.

Once leaving a lake, the scenery was so picturesque Don reached out and knocked on the camper. Zip (Susan) got on the intercom system and said, "What do you want Dad?" Don re-plied, "Look at the Damn." To which Zip replied, "The damn what daddy!?"

Once, Don got a squirrel wounded up in a tree, four miles from home. However, they'd run out of bullets, so Don had his brother run home and come back with more bullets.

One-time Don and some friend decided to go racoon hunt-ing. So, they borrowed a Dog and went out. The funny thing was, they would turn the dog loose and follow him to a tree, running through the woods to get there. At the tree, there would be noth-ing. "Well shit," they'd say. Finally, the dog would get to direct-ing them again. This short but exhausting game lasted all season long. So, they finally went to Cousin Lowell who "knew 'coon hounds." This is when it came to light the dog was chasing rabbits.

"We were on the Missouri river once and he shot a duck," Don began while describing yet another hunting trip. As it hap-pens, Don's cousin who shot the duck, climbed in to retrieve it. "You know, it's a pretty good current," commented Don. Some-times the current being 4 or 5 miles an hour, "He spent half a day getting' that duck by rowing the boat."

Don's cousin Herb bought a dog once called Ace. Ace wasn't much good as Don recalls but, "When pheasant season first opened, you couldn't shoot quail." … "so we shot some quail we shouldn't have, *and* we shot some duck we shouldn't have." They were stopped by a game warden and Don 'fessed up that they had shot some duck and didn't have a duck stamp. "We're not worried about that," the Warden replied, "We're just after those sons of bitches who shot quail." Hearing that and getting a second alone, Don had a quail in his pocket, so he threw it into the brush. "Ace had never pointed a bird in his life and he's over there…" Ace was panting and pointed like it was his job…

They went down the road and Ace pointed a skunk which got him and Don *COVERED* in stink. "I had to spend the rest of the day in the trunk of the car with that damn dog," recalls Don. "It was cold!" he added shivering.

"Another day, it was the longest day of my life." Don had borrowed a gentleman's license who was 6'2" and 220 lbs. If you know, Don, he's lucky to be half that. "It was a horrible day. Every time a door slammed I'd look around. I'd never do that again."

"We were going to western Kansas, the day before pheasant season and Cec, he was a good shot. He was a good shot," Don recalled with a smile. They saw some pheasant which they couldn't shoot until the next morning. "Cec jumped out, I'll get 'em, I'll get 'em, I'll get 'em!" As Cec ran down the field- "All of a sudden from nowhere comes a BIG-ASS HAY-TRUCK!" The truck got up behind Cec and began pushing him. "We talked our way out of that one that was a bad one. I think he got all three of them, out of season, out of limit and out of everything!" Laughing to himself, "I can just remember that big-ass bumper, HELL! It was wide as this room!!!!" Don laughed to himself.

Jim's steering apparatus went out on his boat once. So, he hooked it up, but he hooked it up backwards. "You ever try to steer a boat when it's backward!?" Don asked. "It's a hell of a job!"

"We always had car trouble and it always happened to be near a corn field. So, I'd say, car trouble kids! And they'd all head out into the corn field and we'd have fresh corn the whole dang weekend."

"We were going to the damn about 20 miles away and I got a couple ropes, and a couple kids grabbed 'em to ski all the way down there and back. "We went to one lake, Bull Sholes and I didn't want to drive that weekend/vacation and we figure we drove to Denver just on the water. We went through 12 gallons of gas a day. That was beautiful water down there."

After constant assurance that the kids wanted to tent-camp in the backyard, Don would finally agree. "...And hell, by ten o'clock I'm alone in the thing. One by one they just... ...gone."

One summer, Don and the family had finally bought a camper and went on one of their family get-aways into the vast-ness of nature. Don needed his hands free, so he tucked his keys (to his boat, truck etc.) in his swimsuit. He then used an outdoor toilet where they fell in the hole. Don's solution was, "I called Knuck." Don began to tie knots around his sides and back. The plan, was to send Knuck in. It was at that time, that someone came to use the toilet. "I said it was out of order," Don chuckled to himself. To which the man replied, "How can an outdoor toilet be out of order?" Don just repeated himself. The man got angry and left.

Next, it was voted that this was not a very good idea. Don was still tying knots when someone said, "Landing net" which is a net used to catch a fish when you bring it into the boat. As soon as the new suggestion had been put out, Knuck was gone. The land-ing net worked in retrieving the keys and as Don says, "I washed 'em for a half an hour."

Yinner had a cat she was very fond of, yet Don was not so fond of it. One time, Yinner brought the cat camping with the family and on the first day, the cat went missing. After they hadn't seen the cat all weekend Don was loading the car, when it was time to leave, wondering where the cat was. He then heard very soft meowing. Don began looking all around and followed the sound until he realized, the cat was stuck in the lawn dart box.

"Good Ol' Derek (one of Don's grandsons). I took him fishin' one time" Don began. At one point in the day, Don was fishing off of the back of the boat when the boat began going back and forth, back and forth. Derek was playing with the trolling motor. Don was getting tossed back and forth, "Quit that damnit!" Derek was getting bored as they weren't catching anything. Finally, Derek was allowed to go swimming. After a short while Don turned and saw Derek holding on to a strap that was usually attached to the boat. This strap was for hitching the boat to the trailer for transportation. Suddenly, Derek let go of the strap and Don watched as the strap disappeared into the depths of the lake. "I said, what did you do that for!? And he had no good answer."

"Another story on Derek," Don smirked. Once when hunting, they were in a big long draw between fields. The rest of the hunters were going to move up along the fields while Don hunted on the bottom to draw the birds up with the dogs. Don could hear them breaking brush, then all of a sudden, "woof, woof, woof." "What the hell?" Don thought as he heard more "woof, woof, woof." Don got to counting the dogs to be sure he had them all, he did. "The dogs were with me and Cece told Derek he had to act like a dog because there were no dogs barkin'". Don said, "Derek, you have my permission when you get older to beat the tar out of him!"

"Then we took Will, Alan's son" Don said as he looked off into space recalling the scene. He had the flu and gave it to everyone that went hunting. "We all got sick."

"I don't know if it was Charlie or Charlie's son, shot this bird off this lady's porch; She didn't like that. She followed us for about 20 miles."

"Any good stories with Ray," I asked. "Yeah, one time I was ready to kill him," Don laughed. They had been out at Don's buddy's farm pond. There was a lone goose coming who had clearly been flying a long way off. The goose peeled and Don was over on one side and Cec was over at the other. Here he comes, tree high, perfect shot. Don was getting ready and getting ready when the goose got over where Cec was and **BOOM!** Cec had shot him right out from under Don. "And he missed him, it pissed me off," smiled Don.

Once, when Don and Cece took Al Bauer and his son out to Glen Elder Lake, they were doing a crappie trip. This was an annual trip. The way it worked was some people would go out in the morning then come back in and drop off fish. Others would clean the fish while people went out to catch more fish. "By the time we'd go home we'd have enough fish for a whole year," reminisced Don. The gents (to use the term loosely) went into town for something and on the way back Al began, "oh my God, oh my God!" When asked what happened, Al explained he'd left his wallet at the bait store. Don, in his usual poise of compassion and empathy responded, "Aww shit Al." Al insisted they let him out, all the while claiming that he would hitchhike back to the store then *back* to the campsite. Don disagreed with Al's plan.

At one point, Don got a new anchor for his birthday from his kids. "It was a beautiful anchor," Don smiled thinking back. Don "had it all roped" and he threw it out. Then waited for it to tighten up and stop the boat from moving. However, the boat continued moving until, they ran out of rope. "I couldn't be mad at any of the kids because I did it myself, you know?" Don explained while chuckling.

Once when it was summertime and Don was camping with Charlie, they wanted to start a fire. They poured some gas around the campfire for dinner, "Gas of course is heavier than air" which means it drops down then spreads out. That said, Don and Charlie didn't know that at the time. They lit the fire and the whole area came up in flames. "We got out of there before the flames got us, but it was pretty hairy for a while."

"Charlie had two boys and I had two boys and we went hunting a lot together." One trip, they stayed with another Coast to Coast store owner. For the night, everyone was given space in the basement to stay in. Charlie, however, was afraid to stay in the basement. He didn't like that there was only one exit/entrance to the basement (which describes most every basement) in case of fire. Everyone went out drinking that night and came back to the basement. Don went to bed while the boys were still out running around.

"Early, like two, three or something in the morning," Don recollected "I got woken up." Don had woken up because there was a flashing light in the basement. "What the hell is this?" Don asked as he looked over and saw a highway marker from a barricade. Don looked around and realized there were five of them. The boys had gathered up highway markers from all over town and put them in the basement. It was then Don noticed that the owner of the house and a worker from the highway were there. The man from the highway was looking for his barriers. Don walked up to the boys and lined them up. He then delivered the line of a lifetime, "Did you know I was a magician!?" The boys of course conveyed that they did not. Don continued, "You wanna see a real magic act?" "Yes!" the boys responded. Don went on, "See all these flashing lights? I'm gunna close my eyes and in five minutes I'm gunna open them up again and those lights are gunna be gone." Don laughed to himself, "They were gone..."

"We were hunting Lovewell Lake, and it was cold," Don began. They hit some ducks that fell then floated below the damn. When the guys went down, they saw catfish swimming around in there. Naturally, the guys thought to themselves, "We're liable to get some fish while we're out here hunting." Don and his friends began shooting at the catfish with shotguns. "But they were too far down, we didn't kill any of them…" Don recalled. After a little while, the guys gave up. When they were walking out, they passed by a guy who was walking down to the area they'd left with a rod, reel, and a container with some minnows. "I don't think fishin' is going to be too good down there," Don tried to warn the guy. Not understanding the full scope of what had happened, the man continued saying, "Well, I'm gunna try anyway."

Once, when Don was out doing his normal weekend routine with friends, they had covered the floor of the camper with empty beer bottles. Their method had been to chuck a bottle after emptying it. "It was about chest high," Don said as he laughed to himself. Next, the guys found themselves having to answer to a highway patrolman. "We were just lucky, he was more interested in our safety with the trailer," Don reminisced, "Then they let us go, didn't look in the car. Must have been even with the seat (seatback)."

CHARLIE THE HUNTING DOG

"We'd pull up to a farmer's house and Charlie
would get to whoopin' the farmer's dogs."

"Yeah, I named the dog Charlie, which kinda pissed him off at first" Don chuckled, "him" referring to Don's friend Charlie. Then Charlie (the dog) got to be a good hunter so Charlie would brag that Don named the dog after him. Then Charlie (Don's friend) bought two dogs and named them Don and Lindsay.

At one point, Don was bragging about how tough Charlie the dog was. Charlie the human responded, "Aww hell, my dog would whip him any day." Don replied, "No they wouldn't." Handling their disagreement like the true gentlemen they are, the two men organized a dog fight. "We decided it wasn't a good idea," Don recalled.

When asked about his old hunting dog Charlie, Don would say, "Everyone hated Charlie, except hunters. They would come knock on the door and say, 'hey, can Charlie go hunting?' and I would say, 'Well only if I go with you'!"

Charlie (the dog) loved to fight. The worst part was Charlie didn't care whether he won or lost, he just liked to fight. Once, Don was talking to his neighbor who had a big police dog. Charlie came up and the police dog went after Charlie. The tiff was so bad, the neighbor got on top of his car. Charlie held his own though, partly because he was a sixty-pound Brittany. Large for a Brittany for those who don't know.

According to Don, Charlie was so good, he got birds on public hunting ground.

One year, two or three weeks before hunting season, Charlie got out. After a while Charlie came back to the house with his ear just barely hanging on to his head. Naturally, the tragedy for Don was that Charlie got in a fight just before hunting season. Don promptly put Charlie in the pen. It was at that moment the backdoor neighbor pulled into their driveway and Charlie began to lose his mind, running up, down and all around. Charlie was jumping up and down, throwing himself against the fence as his ear was flopping around all over and blood was being flung all over. Fortunately, for Don, he got Charlie calmed down and they were able to hunt.

On that hunt Charlie mixed it up with a racoon. It was so bad Don was worried Charlie was going to get his guts torn out. As it happens, Don's friend Charlie was with him and pointed his gun at the tussle. Charlie, being a bad shot, drew the response from Don, "Charlie, don't, don't, don't." ***BOOM!!!!***

Don then picked up Charlie by the collar and he looked alright. Don set Charlie down who then took two steps and fell over. Don lowered his head in sadness thinking, "That damn 'coon killed Charlie." Then, soon after, Charlie stood up, shook himself off and proceeded on with the hunt. It was then Don realized, he'd accidentally choked Charlie out when he picked him up by the collar.

Down along the next draw, Charlie (the dog) pointed at another racoon. Don called him off which seemed like a pretty easy task that time around.

Once, Don and the family left Charlie in the house when they went out. Charlie decided to rip through the Christmas presents and numerous decorations. "Now I was pissed off," recalls Don. "So, I got him to his dog pen outside." Don then had the rest of the family in the house voting on whether or not they would keep Charlie. Meanwhile, Don was outside with his shotgun aimed at Charlie, "Do I shoot the son-of-a-bitch or not!?" But God willing (probably not) or by some other miracle (for lack of a better term) Charlie was voted to stay in the family.

Sam was a dog from a litter Charles had had and was the one Charles couldn't get rid of. "He was a little guy, but he was pretty feisty." Sam went out with Charlie the dog and Don on one particular trip. Sam was thinking he was tough like Charlie. Sam got out of a fight on this trip with his tail all chewed up. The poor dog was walking around and yelping and whining. According to Don, "it didn't get any better." Feeling for poor ol' Sam, Don called Klutch and told her she had to take Sam to the vet. "Take Sam to the vet?" Klutch shouted. "Yeah," replied Don. "I can't take my kids to the doctor; I'm not taking a damn dog to the vet!" Klutch responded. At home Don let Sam out whimpering as usual but then he came back in happy as a clam. When Don looked closer, he saw Sam's tail was gone.

"Sam was about as worthless as tits on a boar," recalled Don when reminiscing about the time Ray wanted to take Sam out hunting. While it was normal for Charlie to run off on a camping trip for a couple days and return on his own, Sam once disappeared which prompted a search party. "I thought Cec was going to bust out crying..." Don said. Eventually, everyone piled into the truck/camper. At the sound of doors slamming, they looked back and could see Sam coming down the road. "…He was that close."

"Charlie and the gas-station, that's a funny one," Don said with a smile. A 'quality oil' sat just outside Topeka where they had a manager in a house trailer living next to the gas station. This is where one fateful day Don pulled up with the family on the way out for a family trip. He pulled over to get gas and let Charlie out. "Oh boy," Don said as memory struck. If it didn't move, and few things did, Charlie pissed on it. So, Charlie jumped out of the camper, ran over to the trailer, jumped the fence, pissed on the grill, shook the little tiny dog in the yard then dropped the dog and returned to the trailer. "I was never so embarrassed in my life," Don recalled.

"Hell, he pissed on my bed all the time, not all the time, but just enough to piss me off!" Don recalled about Charlie. "And it pissed me off!" Don added. "Was it just on your side?" I asked. "Oh yeah!" Don answered. "He'd go in my bedroom then look at that then look at me. Charlie! Don't you dare! Charlie! You son-of-a-bitch you'd better not! Then I'd beat the crap out of him!"

I asked Don if he had to train him for hunting and he said no. However, Don said once he almost shot Charlie. "One day we were hunting, a whole bunch of guys." A bird was laying in the bottom of a gulley. Don threw Charlie in to force his hand and they got to walkin'. The other guys remarked at Don's dog and Don said, "You talkin' about my dog?" To which the man replied, yeah.

"He was one hell of a dog!" Don recalled. "Were did you get him from?" I asked. "I bought him. Oh, one of Charles' buddies had a big litter where I got him."

LOVE OF MY LIFE

Don first met Klutch through youth activities. He began by dating a friend of hers. He got turned off from the friend because, "she was bossy." If you're reading this and knew Ruth, you probably laughed out loud just now. Don began dating Ruth instead. "It just kinda happened, it wasn't any lightning bolts or anything," Don explained. Obviously, Ruth was attracted to Don's sensitivity and romantic behavior.

One night, late at night, Don was driving his Model T with Klutch when all of a sudden, BAM! Don looked up and saw his rear wheel go rolling away in front of him. Don jumped out and chased it down as in his words, "the damn thing went a couple blocks". He then put it in a toolbox in the back and called Klutch a cab. "And she stuck with me through all of that, so I figured she was pretty good," Don added.

Don didn't always have all the fun. Don took Klutch hunting one time, "And she was a good ole sport, she tried it," Don remembers. They were hunting squirrel once and Don told Klutch to watch the trees. Klutch put her eyes right up and "They" kept walking. "It seemed like about 20 minutes later and I can't find her," explained Don. Don eventually found Klutch back at the tree where he'd given her the original instruction.

That same trip, Don shot a squirrel that thudded, meaning he'd hit bone and muscle. However, no squirrel. Don's plan was to climb up the tree and shake out the "unfinished" squirrel. At that time, Don had a .410 shotgun and a rifle. He set them next to the tree and told Klutch, "If he comes out, and just sits there, take the rifle and shoot him. If he starts runnin', take the .410 and shoot him." Don climbed up in the tree and got to shakin'. The squirrel fell out and **BOOM!** Don then climbed down as Klutch asked where the squirrel had gone. Don then pointed at the tree and told her to follow his finger. His finger ended up at her feet where the dead squirrel was lying, in which Don thought to himself, "Oh my God, she doesn't know which one to use!"

MISPLACED CIVILIAN

"The title of that chapter will be, 'A Misplaced Civilian';
that's what I was…"

During the Korean War, Don had used College deferments a few times to avoid the draft. "But they caught up with me," Don laughed. He ended up in a reserve unit and deployed to Japan.

In basic training Don had a car. It had to be kept off of post, however. As you can imagine, this did not stop Don. He would sneak off with higher ranking individuals, take the car to the out-skirts of Fort Riley and they would sleep all day. "I qualified on a machine gun and never even saw one."

Once, Don had a meeting to go to, so he locked his rifle up in his locker. "The meeting lasted longer than I thought it would be," Don admitted while thinking back. He returned to his area and found they were looking for a lost rifle. That experience taught Don why the captains go down with the ship, "because they can't afford that damn ship."

"I had the MPs out looking for me on my honeymoon," Don chuckled. Don had asked his new captain if he could take some time off after basic as he was getting married. However, since Don had only been in for eight weeks, he hadn't earned any leave time. The MPs got in touch with Don's in laws who said Don was somewhere down around New Orleans. The MPs then put an APB out on Don. Don and Klutch drove from New Orleans to Kansas City in one day on two lane roads (with 71 highway in Arkansas being a gravel road at the time). Don and Klutch got home to his in-laws where Don had received a telegram. This telegram was appraising Don that he needed to be in Colorado Springs by Midnight, that night. It was already two or three in the morning. In true Don fashion, he went to bed, "What are they doing to do? Kill me? Send me to the Army? What?"

"Take that hill they said," Don could recall. "Hell, if you want it so damn bad *you* take it!"

When Don went to Japan, he had to go by ship. Some MPs were checking people's pockets and bags as they were getting on the ship. "At that time, I was drinking pretty heavy," Don said explaining he had hidden alcohol in his duffel bag. That said, Don put his alcohol in plastic bottles. To save time, the MPs were beating the hell out of the duffel bags with their bats which would reveal if anyone had a glass bottle hidden in their bag. As you would expect, Don's plastic bottles passed the test.

Everyone wanted the bottom bunk going overseas. Coming back, everyone wanted the top. This being because when the guy on the bottom bunk got seasick and puked, they'd be out of the way.

"I got fired from my job on the boat," Don laughed. Don's job was to take the trash in a lettuce crate, up three or four stories and back to the fan tail and throw the trash overboard. Then the sharks would eat it. On a typical day, the fan tail was 60 feet out of the water. On this particular day, Don set the crate down and looked up and up and up. The wave was several feet above the deck. Don promptly returned to the kitchen and told his NCOIC (Non-Commissioned Officer in charge), "Sergeant, you can do what you want with me but I'm not going back there again. That is not a place for a Kansas boy." The Sergeant rolled his eyes and told him to just get rid of it and that he didn't care what Don did to get the job done. Don said okay and returned to his trash. When Don went back outside, he exited on the side of the ship. One deck below it was all open. Not taking nature into account, Don proceeded to dump the trash over the side of the ship. "Well, it was awful windy," Don smiled. All the trash blew back into the deck below which was all Officer territory."

Don was then placed on Chapel duty. "No one used that place the entire time we were there," Don shrugged. But it was warm and out of the wind.

To do laundry on the ship, since there wasn't a laundry service, the men would tie their clothes to rope and let the rope drag in the water. "One time I left mine in too long. I reeled my clothes in and got back two sleeves."

Once Don was on the top deck when an Officer's wife threw an apple or orange out at the troops with attitude like she was throwing scraps to dogs. After this action, the woman turned to walk away. Don picked it up and threw it right at her and struck her in the back. No one turned on Don which allowed the act to go unpunished.

"31 days on that ship. Coming back under the Golden Gate Bridge they could have poured garbage on me and I would have just smiled at them."

"'Lindsay, report to the Officer's Club'. I thought, oh shit, what did I do now?" Don reported and they asked if he had indeed taken some business courses in college. Don explained to me he never admitted to anything like that because in basic some drill sergeants asked who was in college. "A couple of dumb-shits raised their hands…" and the drill sergeants responded, "Then you're smart enough to dig this hole." "I learned pretty quick on that," Don laughed. The Officer's club manager was going back home, and they wanted to know if Don wanted to be club manager. Don knew he had no idea how to run the club, but he did know it was better than what he was doing at the time. They saw Don was hesitant so they reassured him that because he'd be working some evenings on top of day duties, that he would be compensated an extra $50 a month. This is what he was already making, so at the tune of doubling his income, Don agreed.

The first week, they had a Hawaiian Luau. Pig and everything. Don was at the desk at the front door taking people's money. Don's Colonel came in wide-eyed, "Did you charge General (So and So) to come in here!?" Don responded, "Sir if he came through that line, I got him!"

While at the officer club, Don hadn't been keeping books, this went on for months. Eventually, the Inspector General and a couple guys came in and said, "We want to see your books." Don simply replied, "I don't have any books." Don was pretty sure they were going to have a stroke. They ended up saying, "Okay, you have a month. We'll be back in a month and your books better be right." Don smiles telling the story, "And they were right. Every penny was accounted for."

Once a Major had been issued an O3A3 bolt action rifle. He wanted to test it out, so he got Don, a Private First Class. After 15 to twenty minutes of pulling targets for the Major, Don stopped and made the Major switch with him. Don wanted a turn firing the rifle.

One night, Don was wearing a civilian shirt as he headed off base for the evening. The MP at the gate wanted Don to button up his shirt all the way. Don was confused as he was wearing civi's and the rule didn't apply unless in uniform. However, the MP still wouldn't let Don leave until he complied. Don eventually did as the MP said then left.

A week later, that same MP came to the Officer Club to get coffee for a Major. Don told the MP that rules are rules and because the MP was an enlisted man, he was not allowed in the Officer Club. "Pretty soon, here's a phone call. 'This is major So-And-So with the MP detachment.' I said, yes sir, how's your morning? 'It's not worth a damn! What the hell is going on!? I want my GODDAMN COFFEE!' He was pissed off" Don laughed. Next, Don explained his ruling after which the Major made it very clear, he wanted his coffee. In the end, the Major got his coffee.

"Then, our night out. It's got to be truth because I couldn't make this up," explained Don. There was an area that was off limits. Military personnel could not go there, it was known as a tourist trap. Naturally, Don found a buddy as daring as himself and they went anyway. They went by a couple bars and eventually saw one where a guy was waving them in. The two men entered the bar and made it very clear that all they wanted was beer, "beer only." Don continued, "We're sittin' there and then this gal all of a sudden gets up on this bar and starts strippin'... ... and pretty soon she was pretty well naked, you know." Don's friend asked if he'd explained they would not be paying for that and Don replied, "I sure did." But things were not looking good. After a short while Don stood up and said to his friend, "We're going to get out of here." Now, the Japanese around the area knew some English, so Don delivered the previous line in Pig-Latin. "They didn't have any idea what I was talkin' about!" Don laughed to himself, remembering the scene. Don told his friend, "In about five minutes, leave." Don got up and was told not to leave by the staff. Don settled them down explaining he simply had to use the restroom. He then explained that his friend would stay until he came back. The staff found this reasonable and let Don proceed. Don then went outside and peed. The front wall of the building was all bamboo. Don then climbed over the bamboo wall from the "bathroom" and made it outside of the bar. Suddenly, Don heard the "Goddamnedest crash" he'd ever heard in his life. "CCCCRRRR-

RAAAASSSSSHHHH!!!!!!" Don recounted. "It was like a car wreck! Then I looked over and here, the sonofabitch, he'd come through the wall!" Don looked up in disbelief as the girl who'd been stripping was putting on her clothes to join the other staff in giving chase. Don and his friend ran down the street to escape the staff with the police now joining the chase. The two made it to a subway station and ran down the stairs. After a lot of running around they saw and empty booth. Don grabbed his friend and threw him into the booth, "Sit down on the booth and pretend you're asleep." Don now smirked, "Well, you know, all GIs look alike." The police ran right by. After a half an hour, Don looked both ways and he and his friend left.

"The taxi driver, where we went, most every place was 100 yen for the fair," Don recollected. In American dollars at that time was about 26 cents. Don and other GIs would tell the taxi drivers they'd give them 500 yen to take them back to their camp.

Once, when Don was watching the meter, the taxi driver drove until the meter hit 500. Don tried to get the driver's attention to get him to stop but the driver kept going. The driver ignored Don and his friends. Don told the driver to stop so he could use the bathroom outside of the car. The driver argued and refused but Don convinced him. As soon as the driver stopped, the soldiers busted out. "If he'd have taken the 500, we'd have paid the 500. But he let it run up to almost one thousand yen." Don and his fellow soldiers were running fast up to the gate to post. They all got waved through where they ran up to their bunks and pulled the covers over their heads. Next thing they knew, the MPs and the cabbie were going through the room with flashlights looking for the alleged bandits.

"Another one that wasn't real funny. After it was all over, I was scared to death," Don began. Someone had robbed a cab driver and beat him up really bad. For this, the higher-ups had the entire battalion fall into formation. Then, the cab driver walked up and down the aisles looking to point out the man who'd beat him up.

It had not been Don, but as the cab driver reached Don, he stopped. He then looked Don over and up. Keep in mind, at this time, Don didn't even know what was going on or why. After a moment, the cabbie walked off to the next guy and so on and so forth. Once it was over, Don asked someone else what that was all about. They began to explain what had happened, "Well that guy got all beat-up." Don replied, "I saw those bandages and everything." "Well, he's looking for the guy who did it," Don was told. After a brief pause from being struck by the near-miss Don replied, "Well I didn't do it!"

"We had special service hotels. Really nice, they were General's houses and they were overtaken and turned into a rec type hotel. We got to go there often, and you could see Mount Fuji from the front of it. We were all gunna climb it one time, but we got too damn drunk to do it."

Once when on the train to get back to Tokyo, Don and his friends ran into a little Japanese farmer. They happened to have a bottle of Martini's and a fifth of whiskey. When the farmer showed an interest in the bottle Don and his friends gave the man some upon request. The man's requests continued as did their generosity. "...Pretty soon, he was drunker than a skunk." As Don and his friends exited the train, the farmer was still on the train, singing.

DON-ISMS:

Don't name a pig you're going to butcher

Can't tie a good knot, tie a lot of them

If you come to a stump while you're plowing, plow around it

If you're out of shells, nobody in your party shoots your
caliber, but if they run out, it's a perfect match

I drive like the people I used to cuss

Life has gotten so much better since I've given up hope

It's so dry, the trees are lookin' for dogs

That went over like a lead balloon

What's time to a pig?

You are about as funny as a rubber crutch

Are we having fun yet?

Slicker than greased owl shit

I wonder what the poor folk are doing

You are in whompin' range

I'm going to jam your zipper

There is no rain within 500 miles of here

As fine as frog hair

Hang on to your girdles girlies

He was whining like a poisoned pup

I'd like to buy that guy for what he's worth and
sell him for what he thinks he's worth!

Man! It smells like a room of old folk in here!

He's as useless as teats on a bull

You're so slow I have to line you up with a
fence post to see if you're moving

(While Cec was driving) Just try to keep it between the fence lines

You could screw up a crowbar in a sandpile

Never pass up a beer or a piss call

You're trying to cram 3 pounds of s*** into a 2 pound bag

Everybody, put on a coat because your mom is cold

You don't have the sense God gave a goose

Time to piss on the fire and call the dog

When cooking carp, you gotta tenderize it, marinate it
for three days, then cook it on a cedar plank. When it's

done, eat the plank 'cause it'll taste much better

(Asking Klutch) Are we going to go on vacation together, or are we going to have fun?

It's like hitting yourself in the head with a hammer. It feels good when you quit.

Close enough for government work

You know the definition of comedy? Tragedy plus time

It's raining like a tall cow pissing on a flat rock

I'd rather be pissed off than pissed on

I've been trying to leave since I got here

Made in the USA
Coppell, TX
11 December 2022

88371612R00023